Daisy the Doctor

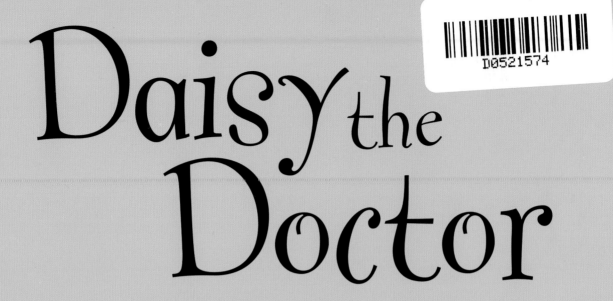

Felicity Brooks

Illustrated by Jo Litchfield

Designed by Nickey Butler

Medical consultants: Kristina Routh MBChB,
Andrew Jordan MBChB MRCGP

This is Daisy the Doctor,
taking her son Ben to school.
After she's dropped him off,
she drives to work.

The traffic can be terrible.

Daisy works at the Medical Center. Her job is to help people stay healthy and to treat them when they are sick.

These are the people Daisy works with:

Alice the Receptionist

Michael the Nurse

Doctor Ashwin Kapoor

The waiting room is already packed with people when Daisy arrives.

Alice hands Daisy a pile of notes about her patients.

Dr. Daisy Flowers

Children can play with toys while they wait to see the doctor. Grown-ups usually prefer to read magazines.

"Good morning," says Alice cheerfully.
"You have lots of patients to see today."

In her office, Daisy checks her computer to see who has appointments.

Daisy's computer is linked to Alice's, so she always knows who's coming to see her.

At nine o'clock exactly, Daisy calls her first patient into her examining room. Do you know his name?

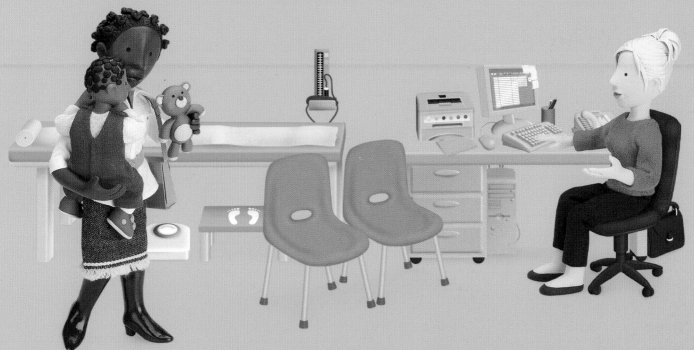

He's a little boy named Isaac Sanchez.

"How can I help?" Daisy asks.
"Poor little Isaac's been up all night with an awful earache," says his mom.

"Big owie!" squeals Isaac, pulling on his sore ear.

Daisy gets out her otoscope to check Isaac's ears. He looks a little worried, so Daisy shows him how to use it on his teddy bear. "See, it doesn't hurt your bear," she says.

Then she looks inside Isaac's ears.

"Hmmm... his left ear's very red," she says. "He has an infection, so he'll need some antibiotics and painkillers."

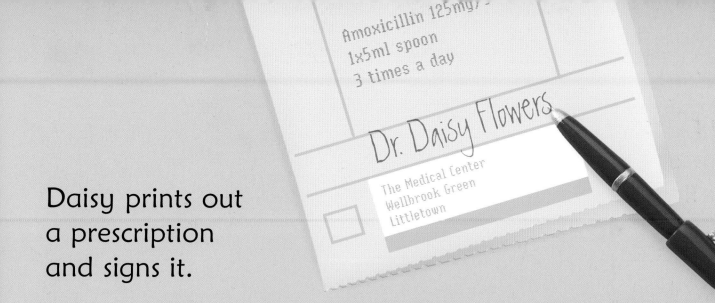

Amoxicillin 125mg/
1x5ml spoon
3 times a day

Dr. Daisy Flowers

The Medical Center
Wellbrook Green
Littletown

Daisy prints out
a prescription
and signs it.

"Please come back and see me in a day or two
if he's not better," she says as she hands the
prescription to Isaac's mom.

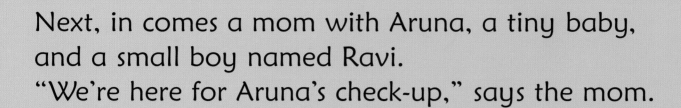

Next, in comes a mom with Aruna, a tiny baby, and a small boy named Ravi.
"We're here for Aruna's check-up," says the mom.

Daisy examines Aruna carefully.

She weighs baby Aruna and asks her mom about how she's feeding and sleeping.

She measures Aruna's body...

...and her head.

She listens to her breathing with her stethoscope.

"Aruna's doing fine," Daisy tells the mom.

Just then, Alice knocks and opens the door from Reception.

"Someone's had an accident!" she says. "Can you see him?"

11

Outside in the waiting room Daisy can hear crying.

A young boy is holding his arm and wailing.

Dr. Daisy F

"His... his arm won't stop bleeding,"
says his mom, out of breath.
"Come right in," says Daisy.

13

"What's your name, young man?" asks Daisy as she leads them into her room.

"A-a-a-lex," sobs the boy.

Daisy comforts Alex and gently examines his arm. "It's a nasty cut," she says, "but you don't need to go to the hospital. Michael the Nurse can treat it here."

"Can you tell me what happened?" she asks.

"I was on... on the yellow swing in the playground," sobs Alex,

"and I tried to jump off, like I always do..."

"...but someone had left a bike there and I... I landed on it – BANG! And it really, really hurt."

OOWW!

15

Alex stops crying. He has to be brave when Michael the Nurse treats the cut.

First Michael cleans the cut with antiseptic and dries it carefully.

Next, he puts little sticky strips across it to help it heal.

Then he puts a dressing on it to keep it clean.

"Try to keep it dry," says Michael, adding a bandage. "And your mom'll need to change the dressing every day."

"But I can still do the play, can't I?" Alex asks anxiously.

"Alex is a pirate in his school play tonight," explains his mom.

"Oh, I think you'll make a wonderful wounded pirate," laughs Michael.

Now Daisy the Doctor is running late
and still has a lot more patients to see:

a shy young boy
with tummyache;

a big bald baby
with a cough;

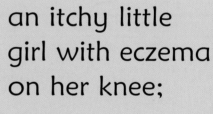

an itchy little
girl with eczema
on her knee;

a boy with
spots on his
tummy;

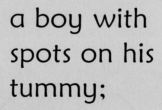

a wheezy girl
who has asthma;

a tall teenager with
a sprained ankle;

a small girl
with a rash...

...and that's not all. Daisy jots down a few notes about each patient.

These are some pages of Daisy's notebook. (She did the doodles too.)

Francesca Lopez - expecting twins
Kate Parker - sprained wrist ☆
Ali Milailo - man with pains in chest
Ruth Levy - aching joints
Isabelle Breux - very bad headache

Lee Chang
Randall Bl
Mairi Mc

When she's seen all of them, at last it's time to go home.

"I'm exhausted," says Daisy to Alice. "I haven't had time for lunch, and I've got a headache."

20

"Maybe you should
see a doctor!" says Alice.

"Goodbye!"

Doctor words

Antibiotic – a type of medicine that kills tiny germs called bacteria.

Antiseptic – a liquid or cream that you rub on skin to kill tiny germs called bacteria and stop infections.

Appointment – If you make an appointment, you arrange to be somewhere at a certain time.

Asthma – If you have asthma, you sometimes find it hard to breathe.

Dressing – a very clean covering for a cut or wound.

Eczema – a rash that makes skin very dry and itchy.

Examining room – a room where a doctor sees her patients.

Infection – when lots of tiny germs called bacteria or viruses get into a part of a person's body and make them sick.

Nurse – someone who helps doctors take care of patients.

Otoscope – an instrument for looking inside a person's ears.

Painkiller – a type of medicine that stops things from hurting.

Patient – a person who goes to a doctor for treatment.

Prescription – a piece of paper signed by a doctor. She writes details about the medicine someone needs on it.

Rash – red spots or patches on skin.

Receptionist – the person at a clinic or medical center who makes appointments.

Sprained – If you have sprained a part of your body, you have twisted or torn parts inside it.

Stethoscope – an instrument for listening to a person's breathing or heartbeat.

Treat – When a doctor treats sick patients, she does something to try to help them get better.

Staying healthy

Here are some of Daisy's tips on ways to stay healthy:

Drink plenty of water.
Two-thirds of your body is made of water, so you need lots to stop it from drying out.

Get lots of exercise.
Exercise is doing things such as playing sports and games, running and swimming. It's good for your body and can be fun too.

Wash your hands.
Always wash your hands before eating or cooking and after using the bathroom. If germs from your hands get into your mouth, they can make you sick.

Stop germs from spreading.
Use a tissue when you sneeze and cover your mouth when you cough. This stops your germs from going into the air and making other people sick.

Try to eat well.
You need a mixture of different foods to stay healthy. Eat plenty of fruit and vegetables every day, along with bread, rice or pasta to give you energy.

You also need two servings of fish, eggs, meat, nuts or beans and two servings of milk, cheese or yogurt to help your bones grow.

Try to eat only a small amount of fatty or sugary foods, such as cakes, chips, sweets and sugary drinks.

Try not to worry.
Worrying about things can make you feel sick. If you're worried about something, tell someone you trust, such as your mom, dad or teacher.

Get enough sleep.
Your body needs sleep to rest and repair itself and your brain works better if you're not tired.

Photography: MMStudios

With thanks to Staedtler UK for providing
the Fimo® material for models,
and to Moir Medical Centre, Nottingham, UK

www.usborne.com
First published in 2004 by Usborne Publishing Ltd.,
Usborne House, 83-85 Saffron Hill, London EC1N 8RT, England. Copyright © 2006, 2004 Usborne Publishing Ltd.